Abstinence Beats Recovery

A compilation of true stories provided by Alcoholics and Drug Addicts about how they got started and the consequences they have suffered. A book written to warn students of the perils of addiciton.

Let's Change the World

A process for becoming a co-worker with Christ to Change the World. Matthew 28:18-20 is your mandate to go and make Disciples of Christ of all nations and Jesus will always be with you.

Let's Change Your Church

A process for becoming a co-worker with Christ to change your church into an Obedience Driven Church. Your church's mission is to change the world.

Let's Change Your School

A process for students to become co-workers with Christ to Change their schools and start a sustained global Christian Discipleship Movement.

Let's Change You

A process for sharing Christ's yoke, to be transformed, and start a sustained, global Christian Discipleship Movement.

Let's Change Your Thinking About Sex and Marriage

How parents and the church must train children about God's reason for sex. Godly sex must be taught from early childhood through marriage.

LET'S CHANGE YOUR CHURCH

*A Process for Becoming a Co-Worker
with Christ to Change Your Church
into an Obedience Driven Church*

*We will Never Change the World by
Just Going to Church!*

John and Dot Overton

Edited by: Will Overton

March 2018

www.equippingstudents.com

WESTBOW
PRESS®
A DIVISION OF THOMAS NELSON
& ZONDERVAN

WestBow Press books may be ordered through booksellers or by contacting:

WestBow Press
A Division of Thomas Nelson & Zondervan
1663 Liberty Drive
Bloomington, IN 47403
www.westbowpress.com
1 (866) 928-1240

ISBN: 978-1-9736-2608-4 (sc)
ISBN: 978-1-9736-2609-1 (e)

Library of Congress Control Number: 2018904628

Print information available on the last page.

WestBow Press rev. date: 04/19/2018

Dedication

To the many frustrated Pastors and Christian church leaders whose church has moved past a plateaued stage and now is into decline.

Acknowledgment

We use The Barna Group as our source for statistics and Christian classifications throughout this book. Post-Christians are those who have left the church though many have also left Christianity. The Barna Group <u>www.</u> <u>Barna.org/research</u>.

Let's Change Your Church
(Into an Obedience Driven Church)

How to Change Your Church to become an Obedience Driven Church

If you are a Pastor:

And you want your church to make a much bigger spiritual impact on your community, you will need to become better informed about your community and focus on improving it rather than using your resources to increase the size of your church. You must have the blessings of God and that is attained by obedience to God. Your priority must be to equip elders and boomers to disciple parents and students.

If you are a Staff Member:

And you want to change your church to have more spiritual effectiveness on her members and her community, you should boldly proclaim the need for an obedience driven mindset and set the pace with your personal example.

If you are a Christian:

And want to change your church to have more spiritual impact on you, your family, and your community, start a more disciplined lifestyle by becoming Christlike and aggressively acting on the obedience assignments in this book.

All must forsake good traditional projects and focus on the Best - Obedience to Christ. Your church can be more active as a spiritual influence in her culture. Work to break down barriers of separation between Christian denominations, ethnicities, and economics. Download and apply the obedience assignments in the free copy of **Let's Change Your Church** workbook from www.equippingstudents.com.

Author's Introduction

We began a search for books
on how to restore failing
churches and found none!

We were members of
the same church for forty-
seven years. During that
period, we served in most
all of the roles of ministry
and lay leadership. The
membership swelled to over 400 active participants
followed by a slow but deliberate decline. We tried to justify
our situation by reasoning that we had plateaued. We could
not accept the plateaued mindset when the population of
our community was visibly growing all around us.

Emphasis was placed on evangelizing non-Christians;
inviting acquaintances to attend church services,
and encouraging them to become church members.
New church members were urged to help operate the
administrative and physical functions of the church by
ushering, taking up offerings, singing or participating in
praise bands, serving on committees, and visiting guests
to encourage them to return to the church meetings. Staff
was hired to entertain youth so they and their families
would continue attending.

Preprinted Bible studies were purchased and taught each week in classes divided by age groups. The Bible was taught but not obeyed! No one was being held accountable. Obedience would have resulted in radical improvements in individual and corporate effectiveness in the community where our church was located.

Christian discipleship was omitted!

Part I

The Problem (As we see it):

Barna Group research shows that 28% of post-Christians are Elders (over age 70; this is the resource age God has placed in your church). Being retired, they have time, experience, wisdom, and wealth. 35% of post-Christians are Boomers (ages 51 to 69; they have raised their children and should take the mantle of Christian leadership). 40% of post-Christians are Busters (ages 30 to 50; they are the most influential with the next generation), and 48% of post Christians are Mosaics/Millennials (ages 13 through 29; the future of Christianity!)

What is the Church and what is Her Purpose?

Before we go any further, let us make sure we agree on what the Church is as well as her purpose in the community.

The Church (with a capital C) is the universal collection of people throughout the world that practice the lordship of Jesus Christ. The church is people. The Church is not an institution, denomination, building, or location. The true Biblical Church is the Body of Christ made up of many members with Christ being the Head. The Church is mystical and united in spirit and truth.

She is a living organism rather than an organization. Thus, the health of the Church requires spiritual nourishment. Small staffs are hired to manage our churches and elders and boomers are not being equipped to perform the critical ministries of the church. Busters and mosaics are not becoming abiding Disciples of Christ.

Too many Christian families are dysfunctional and their children are not being raised in the love of Jesus.

The purpose of the Church is to equip Disciples of Christ, to sustain the work started by Jesus. She is to change the world.

It is unfortunate that throughout the centuries since Christ empowered her with the Holy Spirit men have substituted their rules, traditions, and policies for Christ's commandments and commissions. The local church should be simple in organization and focused on her first love, Jesus the Christ.

Christian information is worthless unless it is applied in faith. Your church must be changed into an obedience driven church if she is to impact your community and the world as Jesus intended.

Obedience Assignment: ☐

1. Write the purpose of your church

Here we are 21 centuries after the initiation of the Church and she has been fragmented into multitudes of denominations, cliques, and cults.

Today we depend upon secular ways of running our churches with CEOs as the head supported with boards governed by autonomous sets of policies and procedures.

Since we no longer depend upon Christ as the head of our churches, Ichabod (The Spirit has left) has been written across the doorposts of our buildings and the Holy Spirit is rarely, if ever, consulted regarding her administration or operation!

Churches are no longer places where you experience God's presence in the company of His people. Sadly, a surprisingly large number of unchurched people tell us that, despite all the attractive programming they have experienced in church, the one thing they are seeking is a powerful, undeniable encounter with the living God – and they have not found it!

People do not come to church for entertainment. Few congregants consider the event to be special; it seems instead, a preplanned, predictable routine.

People come to the worship show without really connecting in a loving way with other believers; the service is essentially just a lubricated machine that tries to impress people every week.

Consumerism is the cultural mindset and the church caters to it!

One thing Barna hears from churchless and churched people alike is that they intensely desire the local church to provide what no other group can offer: An experience of the manifest presence of God.

A majority continue to believe that a meaningful relationship with God is worthwhile. Focusing on building that bridge is much more important, initially and eternally, than signing up another body for membership.

Every church is different, but there are some common elements that leave people feeling empty: these need to be reexamined!

The music portion of corporate worship feels more like a performance than a heartfelt offering to or proclamation of God.

The teaching is designed to inform people about God rather than to usher them into His Presence_and enable a comprehensible Connection with Him.

Public prayers seem more like scripted statements than an authentic conversation with God. They have become more like an extension of the teaching time and are directed to the congregation rather than to the Lord.

The offering is a routine in which people perform their duty rather than eagerly and thankfully returning a portion of the resources God has entrusted to them.

There seems to be no compelling, consistent sense of reverence, awe, gratitude, expectance, or honor associated with the worship activities. Instead, the rituals feel like comfortable habits performed without any expectation of God's presence.

Those peripherals somehow take on a life of their own, crowding out the very Person they are meant to honor.

If we cannot honestly say that we, in community with God's people, meet with Him at the services or events, then we need to reexamine what is getting our attention. If God is not, we are doing it wrong!

These are the Major Reasons You
Need to Change Your Church!

Obedience Assignment: □

> 2. How do you honestly rate your church regarding her obedience to Jesus' commandments and commissions? 1...........10

a. Honestly, meditate on the current state of your church.

b. What would you like the vision of your church to be?

c. Are you willing to propose this vision? You must if you are to change your church!

Part II

The Solution

This part of our book includes specific tasks that you can do to change your church. You must change your mindset from just having people attend your church meetings to this two-step process of equipping the saints and discipling the youth!

Since you are a member of the Body of Christ (His Church) change must start with you. We have incorporated obedience assignments throughout the book for you to obey. Reading and collecting more spiritual information will not result in the changes needed. So please study and prayerfully apply each obedience assignment and check them to  indicate how far you have advanced in preparation to change your church.

Obedience Assignments are also introduced in a Let's Change Your Church workbook available for downloading from our website www.equippingstudents.com

Obedience Assignment: ☐

> 3. Find a secret place away from all human noise to read this book and the Bible daily.

Also read Phase I of our book, Let's Change the World.

The Phase I Curriculum for Christlikeness will prepare you to effectively change your church.

The true church should be an equipping center for training Disciples of Christ that are sent out to make more Disciples of Christ, thus creating a sustained, global, Christian movement. The church was instituted to change the world by joining God's divine conspiricy.

Acts 1:8 instructs you to be witnesses of what Christ has done in your personal life in your neighborhoods, cities, country, and around the world. Most Christians don't witness for Christ because they can't cite anything Christ has been doing in their lives! They are not true Disciples of Christ!

Did you locate a secret place? Your personal obedience is essential to your church change. Do not continue reading until you start obeying.

His Role and Yours

Jesus said that He would build His Church (Matthew 16:18) and commissioned you to make disciples and teach others to obey all that He has commanded you (Matthew 28:28-20). Unfortunately, we too often try to reverse His mandated roles. We work to build our church and fail to make disciples. In other words, we are trying to do Christ's job and fail to do ours. Until this is corrected, your church will continue down the path she is on.

Obedience Assignment: ☐

> 4. Honestly assess your church.
> Is discipleship her priority?
> (Y) (N)
> If No, recommend this change.

Unless the Lord builds the house, the builders labor in vain. Unless the Lord watches over the city, the guards stand watch in vain." (Psalm 127:1).

Jesus has told you to seek His kingdom first and then all other needed things will be provided (Matthew 6:33).

Church overseers should question every 'ministry' and proposed new ministry to identify if they will make Disciples of Christ. If they fail this test, they should immediately be abandoned!

We read of Purpose driven churches, Transformational churches, Simple churches, etc. What is needed to receive the blessings of God is obedience driven churches. Jesus declared that apart from Him, you can do nothing (John 15:5).

What is a Disciple of Christ?

A Disciple of Christ is a disciplined Christian that practices a daily pursuit of Christ. Jesus said, "Whoever wants to be my disciple must deny themselves and take up their cross daily and follow me" (Luke 9:23). New Christians certainly are not accustomed to the lifestyle as Christ's disciples; they must be taught. Such teaching must go beyond the transfer of knowledge into their mind (like Sunday school classes). They must recognize Christ in their teacher and be held accountable to obey their new knowledge. This, in turn, transforms their minds.

Obedience Assignment: ☐

> 5. Tell new Christians about the use of your secret place. Encourage them to find their secret place.

All people, including Christians, have a carnal nature, which craves selfish gratification.

The world system is eager to provide this gratification instantly through the physical senses of sight, taste, sound, touch, and smell.

A Disciple of Christ is somewhat like a worm transformed into a beautiful butterfly. There is absolutely no resemblance between the worm and the butterfly and there is no way to return to the state of being a worm.

Changing your church must start with changing the individuals that make up the church (especially you). They must have a renewed mind. Change is always resisted. A body in motion tends to remain in motion and it takes energy to move a static body. Becoming a Disciple of Christ requires radical change from your cultural norm (especially in your church).

Daily Cross Bearing

In Jesus' day, the Roman government used crosses to execute common criminals. Jesus meant by taking up your cross for you to execute your carnality. Though Jesus never sinned by breaking either civil or moral law, he was falsely accused, abused, forsaken, tortured, and ultimately executed on His cross as if He were a common criminal. While suspended in excruciating pain, He took upon Himself the shame of the sins of the world, including yours!

Obedience Assignment: ☐

> ### 6. Recommend your church study Phase I of the book, Let's Change the World

Jesus did not ask you to take up His cross, but to take up your cross.

Your cross is custom designed to execute your carnal nature with all of its appetite for sensual gratification.

The disciplines of daily cross bearing results in radical changes to one's desires. One's inner focus shifts away from self-centeredness to God-centeredness. God-centeredness makes one want to talk to Him and hear from Him. The agape love resulting from such communion causes a fledgling disciple to want to please Him. Jesus said, "If you love me, keep my commands" (John 14:15).

The commandments and commissions of Jesus are best learned from daily Bible study. You will be used in disciple making if you practice daily prayer during which His Spirit implants His thoughts in your mind.

Jesus commissioned His followers, "All authority in heaven and on earth has been given to me. Therefore go and make disciples of all nations, baptizing them in the name of the Father and of the Son and of the Holy Spirit, and teaching them to obey everything I have commanded you. And surely I am with you always, to the very end of the age" (Matt. 28:18-20).

Obedie-nce Assignment: ☐

> 7. Memorize Matthew
> 28:18-20

Jesus' instructions are very clear, but how to do them is countercultural.
Try as we might through instruction and example, we cannot make a Disciple of Christ! Jesus illustrated how to accomplish everything He commands or commissions; abide in Him (John 15:5). He used a grapevine to represent Himself and branches to represent His followers. If the branch remains attached to the vine, then the ability to bear fruit (be spiritually productive in His kingdom) is possible due to His life flowing through the branch. He goes even further to state that His Father will prune away anything in the branch that hinders fruit bearing so that the branch will become more fruitful.

Branches removed from the vine can do nothing! Such a branch is dead without living vines and is only suitable as fuel for the fire!

With God, all things are possible. Thus, to transform converts into disciples, one must remain attached to or abide in Christ. Disciple making is the job of the Holy Spirit but He uses abiding Christians as co-laborers. You are invited to become a co-laborer by sharing His yoke (Matthew 11:29)

You Must Emphasize Family

God instituted family in the Garden of Eden. The Christian family is made up of a loving husband, supportive wife, and God. If any of these three foundational tenants are missing or minimized, the family becomes unbalanced or dysfunctional.

Obedience Assignment: ☐

> 8. Study Phase II of the Let's Change the World book.

Your church must emphasize family relationships built on Godly foundations. Only then will children be raised in the love of Jesus and not depart from their faith when they mature.

Father absence is an example of profound social change introduced during the 1960s, but is much more common today.

In the 1960s, five percent of live births were to unmarried women. Currently, the percentage is 42%. In other words, today's children are eight times more likely to have come into the world without married parents.

Obedience Assignment: ☐

> 9. Express your love and acceptance of each member of your family.

Mosaics have grown up in a culture that affirms a multiplicity of family types: traditional, blended, nontraditional, and same-sex partnerships. This has influenced their understanding of what it means to be a family, how healthy families should function, what it means to have a good Heavenly Father in their lives, and how they can find meaning, trust, and intimacy in peers, family, and romantic relationships.

Obedience Assignment: ☐

> 10. While in the quietness of your secret place, write an honest assessment of the boldness of your church.

If the parent(s) are not faithful to Christ, the children are not likely to establish a relationship with Jesus either. Children so influenced often become alienated from the institutions of marriage and the church. Many consider their peers as their family, some resort to gangs where they are accepted.

Your church must provide coaches to mentor youth. Show them how to apply Biblical principles in the culture.

Engagements are some of the defining characteristics of the Mosaic generation that are most obvious. They want to re-imagine, re-create, rethink, and they want to be entrepreneurs, innovators, and starters. To Mosaics, creative expression is of inestimable value. The church is seen as a creativity killer where risk taking and being involved in culture are rejected. How can your church peel back the tamper-resistant safety seal, making space for imaginative risk taking and creative self-expression, traits that are so valued within the next generation?

Most churches are perceived as hovering over Mosaics,

protecting them from the sharp edges of cultural life, failure and negative consequences. Whereas they seek freedom and self-expression, your church may have become an over protective way of life in your culture.

This has had a profound effect on church's ability to disciple the next generation of Christians. You should be preparing them for a life of risk, adventure, and service to God. A God who asks that they lay down their lives for His kingdom.

Here are some of the criticisms that young Christians and former Christians level at the church:

- Christians demonize everything outside the church.
- Christians are afraid of pop culture, especially its movies and music.
- Christians maintain a false separation of sacred and secular.
- Christians do not want to deal with the complexities or reality of the world.

The next generation feels as though many Christians characterize every non-Christian thing as bad. For example, they perceive that the church's underlying message about non-Christians, adherents to other religions, atheists, and agnostics, is that these people are categorically evil.

Many young Christians complain that they have been conditioned to fear the world. The problem is that, as they explore the world, they come to believe (rightly or wrongly) that the world is not nearly as hopeless or awful as they have been told. They discover movies, music, and other art and media that sometimes describe the reality of human experience much better than the church does.

Many of the Barna interviews with young Christians focused on the false dichotomy they feel between the church world and the outside world. Research shows that this generation does not see a divide between the sacred and the secular, at least not in the same way their parents do.

To young Christians, the church can feel rigid and unreal. The Christian's black-and-white views do not reflect the world as it really is. "It's complicated" is a phrase heard a lot from young people.

In short, many young Christians feel overprotected. Millions of young believers perceive that the church has kept them fearful of and detached from the world; a world, mind you, that they are called by their faith in Christ to change.

One of the most significant consequences of being overprotected is that millions of young people look for excitement outside traditional boundaries.

Risking holiness does not always have a happy ending, however. During World War II, German pastor Dietrich Bonhoeffer took a stand against Adolf Hitler's Third Reich, and the German church, which ignored and even supported the Nazi regime.

Three weeks after the war ended, Dietrich Bonheoffer was hanged for plotting against the government. He had risked everything to obey in holiness, but God did not "shut the lion's mouths". Bonheoffer's "Daniel moment" got him killed. The widespread, ongoing influence of his life and writings represents a rebuke to a church that had too often failed to prepare the next generation for the grand, terrifying, exhilarating adventure of God's mission to change the world.

Obedience Assignment: ☐

> 11. Emphasize successful marriage with testimonies. Educate mosaics about why God created sexes.

This is the stage of life for developing Godly relationships with members of the opposite gender. If the church does not instruct mosaics on the Godly plan for sex, be assured the culture will teach them perverted expressions of sex.

Your church must assist parents in preparing teens for adult life. Teens must make major life choices about their education, marriage, child raising, and if they will become cultural servants or consumers.

God has placed on parents the responsibility for the transfer of the Christian faith to the next generation. Failure of parents to properly perform  this transference leaves the responsibility with the church. The only other means to make this transfer is the secular world system.

The Christian community must return to Biblical obediance which may be viewed as radical. Jesus was radical! Share Jesus' yoke as your role in the world. Pass the Christian faith to this and future generations.

Obedience Assignment: ☐

> **12. Start a community class on Godly sexuality. Recruit help from other churches if necessary. Offer to help other churches.**

1) Your church needs to reconsider how to make disciples, 2) You need to rediscover Christian calling and vocation: prepare youth for adult life, and 3) You need to prioritize wisdom over information as you seek to better instruct Mosics to know God.

Discipleship must be based on a disciplined relationship with Jesus. Mosaics that will not depart from Christ are promised that Chrisr will never leave them.

You should coach mosaics to become ambassadors for Christ as engineers, medical doctors, nurses, lawyers, pastors, missionaries, pilots, wives, etc. Wisdom is the application of knowledge (Information). You need to prioritize wisdom over information as you seek to know God and instruct mosiacs.

Obedience Assignment: ☐

> **13. Offer a Godly pre-marriage course to your community. Free training presentations and user manuals are available from www.equippingstudents.com**

You should graduate your Elders and Boomers from their classrooms and engage them in the mission for which the church was created in her community. Christian generations are like links in a chain. If parents, elders, boomers, and busters fail in their responsibility, then the next link is broken and future generations are most likely to grow up separated from God and His church. Competing with the world by offering free pizza, playing games, and showing videos to attract crowds is so shortsighted and misleading!

Obedience Assignment: ☐

> 14. Move elders and boomers from Sunday student status to become mosaic mentors.

The haunting question that we must come to terms with is, can't we do something to stop this loss? The answer is YES if you will start a lifestyle of absolute obedience.

You Must Emphasize Youth

If Youth do not establish a genuine relationship with Jesus, they will leave the church when you stop giving out free pizza!

The early church was not a gathering for entertainment and fun; the modern church, too often, teaches youth that is what Christianity is.

Since they are the future of Christianity, youth must be integrated into the core ministries of the church now. Too often youth are separated to themselves and provided worldly, rather than Christian, environments.

Obedience Assignment: ☐

> 15. Recommend your church raise the bar of expectation by providing mosaics with risky opportunities to follow Christ.

They are sometimes shown secular videos, play

games, and are served pizza and burgers in an effort to keep them in attendance at meetings. They are taught to be consumers rather than servants.

Their impression of adult church life is boring and they really do not want to have anything to do with it when they graduate from your youth program.

Obedience Assignment: ☐

> 16. Close the generational gap in both your church meetings and community.

Consequently, when they graduate from their youth group they will, at best, seek another church that offers excitement and programs that they are accustomed to. More often, they just cease going to church to the dismay of church leaders and their parents.

Discipleship and a personal love of Christ has been avoided and the church suffers from a lack of younger Christians moving into leadership roles. Leaders think that they are successful if large groups attend. Just meeting attendance falls short of what we must be doing. Just getting people inside our church buildings is not what we are commissioned to do. Appealing to the consumer appetites of the community to gain larger attendance will not result in a sustained Christian movement!

Youth must be made an important part of the church. They should be given responsibilities of service. For example they should be expected to have an active voice in church ministries and administration. They should be taught the Great Commandment and Commission and shown how to share their testimony with their peers. They should be provided times in the church pulpit to express their Christian life as well as be accountable for their lifestyles.

Obedience Assignment: ☐

17. Include mosaics in the decision-making processes of your church.

Too often, we become complacent if we enjoy a few hundred Christians that regularly participate in our church services. You have not plateaued if the population around you continues to increase while you remain static!

Your Changing Culture:

Christianity is a matter of heart transformation. Unless you bring your Mosaics into a disciplined relationship with Jesus Christ, the world system is going to lure them away.

True Christianity emphasizes faith over reason. The Mosaics in our churches must be taught to, in faith, believe that God is a real Spiritual Person, and He has inspired His written word, the Bible. Unless the Mosaics build their lives on this foundation, they will become vulnerable to the misleading tactics of the culture. True Christianity and the culture are in tension trying to influence each other (and the culture appears to currently be winning!)

Obedience Assignment: ☐

> 18. Encourage mosaics to become co-laborers in leading missional projects locally and distant.

Then he said to them all: "Whoever wants to be my disciple must deny themselves and take up their cross daily and follow me. (Luke 9:23).

The culture says, "You only go around once so gratify self with worldly pleasures and entertainments while you are young enough to enjoy them".

Implying that painting the walls of aging buildings, ushering, taking up collections, and mowing the church grass is all that Christians are called to do is so misleading. Those that do so must surely not be thinking of the future when they will give an account of how they used the resources entrusted to them and how they influenced others.

Obedience Assignment: ☐

> 19. Stop being negative about the world. Instead be positive about missional opportunities to change the world.

Your schools are the largest unreached people group in your community.

Multitudes of students come from dysfunctional families and are poorly equipped to cope with the evil and temptations besetting them.

Every church has easy access to public and private schools but has little, if no, vision for equipping students to become Disciples of Christ.

Obedience Assignment: ☐

> ### 20. Use mosaics to move your church into the technology age.

Students are free to express their faith on their campuses. They effectively communicate with one another using the latest technology.

Obedience Assignment: ☐

> ### 21. Expand your church audio/video room to a church technology studio. Assign mosaics to use the studio to communicate the gospel to peers.

Summer youth camps are often filled with fun and games rather than Christian disciplines. It is so disappointing when they return and provide the church a time of testimony about what camp has meant to them. Rarely do any of the youth mention any spiritual values they have gained at camp but they typically mention all of the fun that they had; thus they really hope their fare will be financed to return next year for another week of fun and games.

A New Technological and Social Reality:

There are over 2,000 registered students in typical US high schools. They are the most vulnerable, unreached

people groups in our neighborhood and are being ignored by the church!

Obedience Assignment: ☐

> 22. Study and apply Phase III of the *Let's Change the World* book.

The secular culture has successfully intimidated the church. The church has surrendered these students to the culture!

Obedience Assignment: ☐

> 23. Coordinate with other churches, local school administration, law enforcement agencies, city councils, etc. to host a community student listening center.

Law forbids Christian adults to evangelize on campus but does not forbid Christian students to evangelize.

Thus, parents and your church must equip these students to share their faith on their campuses. Your church should co-labor with Jesus to start a sustained global discipleship revolution by equipping students.

Digital and mechanical technology, medical research,

conservation, study of the human brain, genetics, physics, and discoveries about our universe shape our reality.

Tools and methods developed by science

significantly affect our daily lives. Our world would be unrecognizable to someone transplanted here from the early twentieth century.

Today's teens and twentysomethings have been more profoundly influenced by these developments than previous generations. Teens and young adults have always lived in a world with email, cell phones, fast food, plastic surgery, cars with airbags, digital music, video, and photography.

They have become encased in a world apart from other people (notice how they seem glued to their smart phones most of the time). Your church needs to provide opportunities for them to talk to peers and elders. Why not use available technology to dialog the gospel across town or to other parts of the world? You must involve your youth in the application of technology to grow the kingdom.

Dialog, creative problem solving, living with questions, group brainstorming, the opportunity to contribute; these are highly valued by the next generation. Technology is available and affordable to interactively teach Christian discipleship around the world without the expense and time required to travel to the remote locations. Internet access is becoming more and more available to all parts of the world.

Obedience Assignment: ☐

24. Start a small student discipleship group using presentation and student manuals available from www.equippingstudents.com

The next generation is living in a new technological, social, and spiritual reality, which can be summed up in three words.

1. ACCESS: The first and perhaps most obvious change relates to technologies.

Young adults connect with each other and obtain information about the world. Hardware such as personal computers, tablets, mobile devices, and smart phones, as well as soft technology like Web pages, apps, etc. are providing the next generation (and the rest of us) with nearly unlimited access to other people and their ideologies and worldviews at the instantaneous click of a mouse or swipe of a finger.

The heightened level of *access* provided by these tools is changing the way young adults think about and relate to the world, their faith, and spirituality through screens.

Simply put, technology is fueling the rapid pace of change and the disconnection between the past and the future. The Internet and digital tools are at the root of a massive disruption between how previous generations relate, work, think, worship, and commit to missions.

Young Christians can create new venues for the Gospel via new media, the Internet, podcasting, blogging, and tweeting, among many others. There is something embedded in their DNA that seeks a platform for influence and advocacy. Your church should capitalize on this resource.

Obedience Assignment:

> 25. Are you familiar with current technology? (Y) (N) If not, befriend a Christian mosaic that is.

If you are not familiar with current technology, seek out a Mosaic or two that are.

Obedience Assignment: ☐

> 26. Spend time with a mosaic in discussions about formation of a Christian technology venue.

Recruit them to discuss true Christianity and to help you set up a Christian network with their peers.

Some have compared the proliferation of these new technologies to the invention of the printing press, which accelerated access to ideas in many ways.

The printing press enabled the rise of science, capitalism, modern political theory, and so much more. Martin Luther described the printing press as "God's highest and extremist act of grace, whereby the business of the Gospel is driven forward".

The digital world with the worldwide Internet may be God's new highest and extremist act of grace.

2. ALIENATION: The second cultural shift is how alienated today's teens and young adults feel from the structures that undergird our society. We might think of alienation as very high levels of isolation from family, community, and institutions.

Alienation is rooted in the massive social changes that began in the 1960s: The civil rights movement, student riots and unrest, the Vietnam War, hippie culture, rock 'n' roll, women's liberation, birth control and the sexual revolution, personal computer technologies, the moon landing, Watergate, FM radio, the Catholic transition to the English Mass, etc.

In many ways, what we now know as "youth culture" was born during that era, as young people embraced new forms of music and art, unprecedented lifestyles, and anti-establishment thinking.

The generation gap is bigger than ever, but it is also a continuation, a deepening, of the rifts introduced by the youth culture of the 1960s.

Obedience Assignment: ☐

> 27. Become a good listener. Encourage discussions about family, school, and church relationships.

Research by the Gallup organization, that stretches back to the 1930s and '40s, shows that young adults first began to act much different religiously from their parents during the 1960s.

The implication of this research is that the dynamic of church disengagement during young adulthood was crafted by the boomers. Now their children and their children's children are taking a similarly circuitous route.

Each generation has taken a longer, path to adulthood. Many young adults are postponing the complete transition to adulthood. This is characterized by five key developmental tasks: leaving home, finishing school, becoming financially independent, getting married, and having a child.

As much as anything, this cultural change marks the gap between church and the lives of today's next generation. Most churches and parishes are simply not prepared to minister or disciple those taking a nontraditional path to adulthood.

Obedience Assignment: ☐

> 28. Explain the difference between being "religious" and being a Disciple of Jesus.

Mosaics often see religious services as time consuming with little or no benefits.

Explain the great difference between being religious and being a devoted follower of Jesus. Share your personal relationship with Jesus with them.

Assure them that they can join Jesus as a co-conspirator to change your church into one that accepts their peers and helps equip them for a quality life.

Another alienating cultural change launched by the Boomers and amplified in the Mosaics is skepticism about institutions. Many young adults feel lost from our systems of education, economics, and government. Many have resorted to drugs and gangs to fill their sense of lostness.

The mosaic generation is skeptical, even cynical, about the institutions that have shaped our society, and while they retain an undiminished optimism about the future, they see themselves creating that future mostly disengaged from the institutions that have defined our culture so far.

The bad news for the church is that, where congregations and parishes are structured to meet the needs of the old normal, it will be difficult for young people to find a meaningful place.

The good news, however, is that the true church is uniquely called to be the community of God; a true, authentic community that banishes isolation, loneliness, and alienation and replaces them with love.

3. AUTHORITY: There is a new spiritual narrative on the rise that says Christianity is no longer the "default setting" of society. The Christian faith exerted significant influence on our culture in previous generations, but much of that public role has dissipated strongly in the last fifty years. Today's mosaics question all authority, even God!

Six different arenas of culture once contributed to the socialization of faith: community, church, religious programming (such as Sunday school), public schools (which had prayers and Bible reading), popular entertainment (which was based, at least somewhat, on a Biblical worldview), and stable family structures. In other words, while far from perfect, Christianity was the culture's autopilot.

Many of those socializing forces have eroded or at least significantly changed. The education system does its best to be religiously neutral and to instill "values" but not Biblical morality.

Obedience Assignment: ☐

> 29. Share the full meaning of Matthew 28:18-20

Share Jesus' claim that He has all authority in heaven and earth and that He will always be with Mosaics that follow Him.

The mosaic generation is growing up in a culture in which the authority of the Christian community and obedience to scriptures are much less present in their development experiences. Mosaic Christians face an environment in which Christianity's authority has been greatly diminished in both obvious and subtle ways.

Students interviewed by The Barna Group had nothing

negative to say about their parents or the Bible but they also saw little connection between these sources of authority and their attitudes or behaviors.

The type of shallow faith that most young Christian people embrace does not require the nurture of a faith community to thrive. The unique take on faith among young Christians is a core reason so many of them are disengaging from the church. The following perceptions represent what some young Christians maintain:

- Church is boring - 31%
- Faith is not relevant to my career or interests - 24%
- My church does not prepare me for real life - 23%
- My church does not help me find my purpose - 23%
- God seems to be missing from my church 20%

Most young Protestants and Catholics do not recall having a meaningful friendship with an adult through their church, and more than four out of five never had an adult mentor.

You have a shallow faith problem because you have a discipleship problem.

Obedience Assignment: ☐

> 30. Interview mosaics about their faith and their relationship with Jesus as an authority figure.

Invite one or two mosaics to join you for burgers and fries. Ask them to discuss their faith and their relationship with Jesus as an authority figure in their lives. Share your attitude about His authority in your life.

We have Christian camps, Christian media companies, Christian schools (from daycare to graduate schools), local churches, and the most advanced communications technology and media that have ever been known to humankind.

However, compare the effectiveness of today's Western church to Jesus' work with His disciples, which were characterized by life-on-life mentoring and apprenticeship.

Should you conclude that by embracing an industrialized approach, your church can improve on the Lord's results?

Discipleship cannot be mass-produced! The apostle Paul instructed his student, Timothy, "Let no one despise you for your youth, but set the believers an example in speech, in conduct, in love, in faith, in purity" (1 Timothy 4:12).

You must mentor your mosaics to the state of maturity where they set good examples to their peers. You must provide them with opportunities to do so in your church rather than isolate them. Your church must change into an equipping center rather than maintaining the status quo!

Most mainline and Catholic parishes have a ceremony for young teens called confirmation, the "sacrament of maturity". The majority of evangelical churches lack such a rite of passage completely, though they may have an occasional youth service when teens are invited to lead the congregation in worship.

Yet, many do not follow the ceremony with a meaningful expectation that the confirmed will contribute to the spiritual growth of the church and community.

Barna's research shows that most young people lack a deep understanding of their faith. The trend of Biblical illiteracy, which is problematic among most age groups, has been on the increase. Most teenagers embrace beliefs that are Christian on the surface, but once you dig a little deeper, you find they are not quite orthodox.

Mosaics should become responsible for participating, and commensurate with their abilities, in decision making and leadership of your congregation.

Why not have mosaics go with an elder or boomer to visit the sick or church shut-ins? Why not teach them to become a "big sister" or "big brother" to younger students; mentoring and discipling their spiritual growth?

Your church must raise the spiritual expectations of Youth if she is to be sustained!

Parents who show by their actions, that the practices of their faith are vague, unimportant, or only tenuously relate to daily life, produce teenagers whose faith is vague, marginal, and unlikely to shape their actions and plans in any significant way.

The vast majority of young churchgoing Protestants and Catholics never receive a sense of how the Bible applies to their calling or interests. Only a small minority discovered a mentor in their faith community, and few ever had helpful coaching from religious leaders pertaining to their educational choices.

Most students who are likely to experience loss of faith do so before college; they begin to feel disconnected from their faith or from the church even before high school ends! Thus, a firm foundational relationship with Jesus must be established as a child, teen, and young adult.

Who will teach Mosaics about Sex?:

Family relationships, parenting, equipping children for marriage, etc. are all dependent upon proper understanding about God's plan for sex.

Sexuality is one of the greatest expressions of God's creativity and of His intention for human flourishing.

Among many of those with a Christian background, the perception is that the church is out of step with the times. They view the church as repressive, controlling, joyless, and stern when it comes to sex, sexuality, and sexual expectations.

- The church's teaching on sexuality and birth control are out of date or totally absent. - 40%
- I do not want to follow all the church's rules. - 25%
- I want more freedom in life and cannot find it in church. - 21%
- I have made mistakes and feel judged in church. - 17%
- I have to live a "double life" between my faith and my real life. - 12%

Chastity and fidelity are significant features of spiritual and sexual wholeness. They emerge from an understanding of God's revelation in the Bible.

Early media (movies and TV) used discretion when

sexuality was even suggested. Remember the I Love Lucy bedroom scenes?

Mosaics are now subjected to a radically open portrayal of sexuality. Thus, their worldview has been influenced by a "sex is about me" mindset. The church is shocked by this cultural change and ill equipped to deal with it; so the tendency is to ignore it.

Most Christians will say that their faith is a relationship with Christ, not a laundry list of duty-bound obligations. Performance Lists are legalistic religion!

Acceptance:

A fence around a church building suggests Keep Out!

No compromise has been the slogan of the Western church, but it does not make sense to the next generation, for whom negotiation and cooperation are facts of life.

This generation needs to see you live as if the Bible has a claim on your life.

Where you discover the clear teaching of God's word, you need to be willing to pursue its role in every facet of your life.

A hallmark of the next generation is their emphasis on fairness over rightness. Teens and twentysomethings tend to determine the rightness and wrongness of their choice by what seems fair, reasonable, and accessible.

Digital piracy is not right, but music sharing seems fair. Many young people are redefining their ethical decisions by what seems fair, rather than by an outside standard of right and wrong.

Never say, I love you because you know you should. Say it because you really love them.

Mosaics can spot a hypocrite and it turns them away.

Your Church is to be on the Offense

And I tell you that you are Peter, and on this rock I will build my church, and the gates of Hades will not overcome it (Matthew 16:18). This one verse quotes Jesus as saying that He will build His Church and the defensive gates of hell will not be strong enough to withstand her bold aggressiveness.

Obedience Assignment: ☐

31. Do your church members actively portray Christ in your community or do they retreat to safety and comfort with their Christian peers?

Is your church boldly proclaiming the Gospel in your community or has she retreated into a defensive position of just trying to sustain herself?

If this is your case, you must actively act to change her. Your church's influence on mosaics is determined more by her actions than by her teachings.

Assess your damage

Before attempting to rebuild anything, you must first assess the condition it is in. This applies to wrecked automobiles, sicknesses, failing businesses, churches, etc.

Since you are focusing on changing your church, make a review of some of the typical paths or traditional habits that have led to the present condition of your church.

The journey of the gospel from the time of Jesus to the present day has encountered a number of well-worn and dangerous paths that are seemingly impossible to avoid.

Because of their deadly nature, it is critical that you be aware of them and attempt to avoid traveling on them as much as possible.

Path 1: Separating from culture like Pharisees

In Jesus' day, Pharisees were a very zealous and conservative sectarian movement that Paul had been a part of prior to his conversion. They were highly committed to getting back to the scriptures and their brand of hard-line religion. They developed a set of laws to separate themselves from others in an effort to maintain their purity and righteousness by living in their own isolated culture. The Pharisees basically believed that they were good and clean before God, so they looked down on everyone else and conveniently overlooked their own sins and hypocrisy. Churches travel this path whenever she imposes man-made rules on people in the name of achieving holiness by avoiding sinners and hiding out in a Christian culture.

You travel this path whenever you hold a self-righteous and judgmental attitude that sees the sin in others but not in yourself.

Sadly, many people despise Christianity because all they have known are arrogant, self-righteous, and judgmental people claiming to be Christians, who avoid them as if they were infected and do little more than yell at them to be moral when they should be explaining how to be redeemed.

Path 2: Blending into culture like Sadducees

Churches travel this path today whenever they do not take sin and scripture seriously. They also travel this path whenever being approved by a culture becomes more important than being faithful to God. Lastly, this well-worn path eventually leads to universalism in which every religion leads to salvation and in which there is little, if any, distinction between true and false gospels. This includes the churches that promote themselves as "open and affirming", which is Judas-talk for pro-Bible compromise.

Path 3: Ruling over culture like a Zealot

Today this form of Christianity exists in both the religious right and religious left. It is present wherever people are more interested in sermons about legislative politics than in sermons about sin and repentance, wherever people get more excited about elections than Easter, wherever more people sign political petitions than sign up to minister, and where people believe that if we simply elect more people like us, the world will be a wonderful place.

Path 4: Ignoring culture like an Essene

This form of consumer Christianity exists wherever people seek out spiritual highs like a junkie needing a fix, wandering from church to church and event to event hoping to be touched by God through the latest anointed spiritual bartender.

The Essenes were not concerned with being separated from the culture like the Pharisees, or with cultural relevance like the Sadducees, or with political power like the Zealots. Instead, they wanted to personally encounter God in spiritual experiences. To accomplish this, they withdraw from society, deny themselves pleasure, and live free from distractions in monkish privacy so they can have mystical encounters with God.

Problems with each of these Paths:

The problem with each of these paths is that they are ways of seeking godliness, as they define it, rather than as God defines it. However, the things that those who are stuck in them desire (holiness, cultural relevance, social transformation, spiritual experience) cannot be brought about by legalism, liberalism, legislations, or becoming monks. Instead, they are the natural effects of faith in the powerful gospel and come from God alone to those who are about His business.

How to Treat Candidate Church Members

To restore declining churches, more attention must be given to discipling new candidates for membership than trying to prevent older members from leaving through the "back door!"

Obedience Assignment: ☐

> 32. Download a free copy of *Let's Change the World* from our website and make copies of Phase I for new church members

Candidates for membership must be nurtured by making sure they are born-again spiritually. They need to fully understand what the church expects from them (biblical expectations) and what they can expect from the church.

They must be taken through a basic discipleship course and assimilated into a small group for additional encouragement.

A curriculum for Christlikeness must be instituted as the most important ministry of the church for new members.

Each new candidate should be instructed to select a secret place where they daily commune with our loving God. They should be instructed to spend daily time reading their Bible and praying.

Discipleship training must not be limited to just classroom instructions and homework assignments. The new Christian must be placed in situations where he or she will experience what has been taught and be held accountable for their faithfulness. A mentor will need to take them along and demonstrate, like in a laboratory, how to share the transforming effect Christ has made in his or her life and encourage non-Christians to practice the disciplines of daily Bible study and prayer. If your church does not have a curriculum for Christlikeness, please download a free copy of our book, *Let's Change the World* and use Phase I (www.equippingstudents.com).

Communicate God's Vision, Not Yours

Clear and complete communication of God's vision, for your church is necessary. All members must have full knowledge of church plans and expectations. Lack of knowledge always leads people to speculate about what is going on and speculation results in rumors and gossip. Rumors and gossip result in confusion and there must be no confusion in the church.

Pulpit announcements are only heard by those present. Printed bulletins are only read by those present to receive them, signage and websites are viewed by few and confidence in their currency and correctness is suspect if not diligently monitored and updated. The lifestyle and witness of members about your church is the most effective communication.

Does God Promise Revival?

There is a great difference between revival and spiritual awakening: a revival occurs when Christians return to their first love of Jesus the Christ. It is a restoration from a state of apathy to a state of true spirituality. An awakening is a community-wide awareness of the need for spirituality. A revived church will often be used by God to bring about an awakening in her community.

The unrevived church is a lukewarm abomination to the Lord and it is His desire above all else to revive and awaken her from her slumber. A lukewarm church actually repels people in the community rather than attracting them. The community sees the lukewarm church as self righteous and judgmental.

To imply that God does not desire to send revival is to indicate that He wants His church to remain apathetic and ineffective. Revelation 3:20 pictures Jesus standing at your church door knocking. The door only has a knob on the inside so He patiently waits for those inside the church to give Him entrance.

Church revival will not start on a corporate level! It will start with individual members (you) who, in turn, will effectively influence other members. Thus, to revive church, if my people, who are called by my name, will humble themselves and pray and seek my face and turn from their wicked ways, then I will hear from heaven, and I will forgive their sin and will heal their land. We are promised in II Chronicles 7:14 that such individuals will be forgiven of their sins and their land (churches) will be healed.

You must believe that God wants to heal your land even more than you do! You do not wait for Him to bring about such healing, He is waiting on you. Your land will not likely ever be healed until your church is healed and that will happen one member at a time.

The revival ball, so to speak, is in your individual court! Want to see revival in your churches? Then humbly seek His face and request that His Spirit well up within you, displacing self from your throne.

Jesus commissioned you to be His worldwide witness and to make disciples of all nations. If you are not being obedient, you are seeing the results of your disobedience! Having met the elders, busters and mosaics, and explored their perceptions of the church and Christianity, the Christian community must be willing to seriously re-examine how they are conducting church and her leadership must be willing to make adjustments. Your focus must be on the kingdom rather than just adding new members to your local church.

Concluding Summary

1. Your church must make an honest survey of how she is using her financial and personnel resources (equip the Saints to disciple the mosaics).
2. Your church must educate herself in the perceptions of the community around her.
3. Your church must focus on Mosaics and integrate them into all phases of church life.
4. Your church must be willing to drop traditional processes and programs, if necessary, to concentrate on the obedience assignments in this book.
5. Your church should reach out to struggling churches by sharing resources. Small declining churches cannot implement the recommendations of this book alone!

All resources for changing your church is available for free downloading from www.equippingstudents.com

About the Editor:

Will Overton, John and Dot's grandson, is a Baylor University senior preparing to receive his Bachelor of Arts degree in Professional Writing

Printed in the United States
By Bookmasters